BRIGHT IDEA BOOKS

ANIMAL CONTROL Officer

by Lisa Harkrader

CAPSTONE PRESS
a capstone imprint

Bright Idea Books are published by Capstone Press
1710 Roe Crest Drive, North Mankato, Minnesota 56003
www.mycapstone.com

Library of Congress Cataloging-in-Publication Data
Names: Harkrader, Lisa, author.
Title: Animal control officer / by Lisa Harkrader.
Description: North Mankato, Minnesota : Bright Idea Books, an imprint of
  Capstone Press, [2019] | Series: Jobs with animals | Audience: Age 9-12. |
  Audience: Grade 4 to 6. | Includes bibliographical references and index.
Identifiers: LCCN 2018035984 | ISBN 9781543557824 (hardcover : alk. paper) |
  ISBN 9781543558142 (ebook) | ISBN 9781543560442 (paperback)
Subjects: LCSH: Animal welfare--Juvenile literature. | Vocational
  guidance--Juvenile literature. | Dangerous animals--Control--Juvenile
  literature.
Classification: LCC HV4708 .H374 2019 | DDC 636.08/32--dc23
LC record available at https://lccn.loc.gov/2018035984

Editorial Credits
Editor: Meg Gaertner
Designer: Becky Daum
Production Specialist: Dan Peluso

Photo Credits
AP Images: Elisha Page/Argus Leader, 17, Hugh Carey/The Wyoming Tribune Eagle, 24–25, Joshua McKerrow/Capital Gazette, cover, Joshua Polson/The Greeley Tribune, 6–7; iStockphoto: crisserbug, 31, hbrizard, 5, IG_Royal, 20–21, imagepointphoto, 18, inhauscreative, 10, 28, lesliejmorrie, 12–13, NNehring, 14–15, Solange_Z, 20, Steve Debenport, 9, ymgerman, 23; Shutterstock Images: afarland, 27, Katoosha, 11, Somwang Asawinulankul, 18–19, Thanarot Ngoenwilai, 26

Printed in the United States of America.
PA48

TABLE OF CONTENTS

CHAPTER 1

ANIMAL CONTROL
Officer

A woman pulls her truck into a parking lot. She gets out. She is wearing a uniform. She greets a man who is standing by his car. The car's hood is open. A **stray** cat has climbed into the engine. The man does not want the cat to get hurt.

The woman is there to help. She puts on leather gloves. She pulls the cat from the engine. She puts the cat in a pet carrier. The woman is an animal control officer.

Sometimes animals get stuck in strange places, such as car engines.

5

ANIMAL HELPER

Animal control officers help stray and wild animals. They help pets that are lost or hurt. Scared animals can bite and scratch. Animal control officers risk injury. But the work is also **rewarding**. Animal control officers make sure animals are safe. Do you like helping animals? Maybe a job as an animal control officer is for you.

Animal control officers sometimes grow close to the animals they rescue.

CHAPTER 2

THE
Work

States and cities have laws about animals. The laws keep people and animals safe. Animal control officers make sure people follow the laws. They also teach people about animals.

Sometimes they give talks to large groups. They talk about animal laws. They teach people how to care for animals. They tell people how to stay safe around animals.

Officers talk to students about how to properly take care of pets.

TAME ANIMALS

Animal control officers protect tame animals. They pick up strays. This includes stray cats, dogs, and other animals.

Animal control officers reunite pets with their owners.

Some owners abandon their animals.

Some stray animals are lost. Others do not have homes. Animal control officers help lost pets find their owners. They take homeless animals to animal shelters.

Some people do not take care of their pets. They may hurt their pets. They may not feed their pets. They may keep their pets outside in harsh weather. Animal control officers check on these animals. They may take away hurt animals. They bring the animals to animal shelters. Hurt or sick animals go to a **vet**.

SAFE SPACES

Officers check on animal care places. They inspect animal shelters and clinics. They make sure places are clean and safe for animals.

Animal shelters take care of animals until they are adopted.

Officers hold down a rescued sea lion to give it medical care.

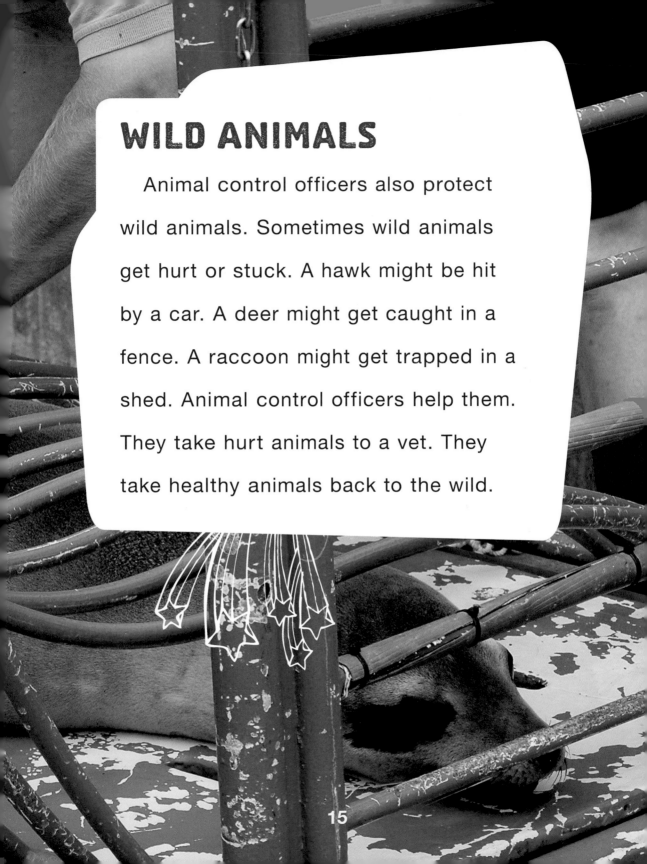

WILD ANIMALS

Animal control officers also protect wild animals. Sometimes wild animals get hurt or stuck. A hawk might be hit by a car. A deer might get caught in a fence. A raccoon might get trapped in a shed. Animal control officers help them. They take hurt animals to a vet. They take healthy animals back to the wild.

CHAPTER 3

THE
Workplace

Animal control officers work outdoors much of the time. Most of them have trucks. They **patrol** for stray animals. They get calls from their offices about animal problems. They drive to check out the problems.

An officer brings a lost pet back to its owner.

Officers use a special pole to catch stray dogs.

Animal control officers' trucks have pens in the back. They can put animals in the pens. They drive homeless pets to animal shelters. They take wild animals back to nature.

THE TOOLS

Officers keep tools in their trucks. They have nets, leashes, and medicine. The tools help them catch animals and take care of them.

Officers often use thick gloves for handling wild animals.

INDOORS

Sometimes animal control officers work in an office. They write reports. They answer the phone. People call the office to report problems with animals.

Some stray animals are sick, weak, or hungry.

Stray animals may live in unsafe areas.

People who break animal laws may need to go to court. Animal control officers **testify** in court. They tell the people at court what they found out about the animals.

CHAPTER 4

GETTING the Job

Animal control officers need a high school diploma. They also need a driver's license. Many officers have experience working with animals. Some officers go to college.

Many animal control officers get special training. They learn about caring for animals. They learn about catching animals. Officers earn a **certificate** at the training.

Officers learn about different methods of catching animals, including how to use cages.

ON THE JOB

Most animal control officers work for a city or county. They make $30,000 to $40,000 per year. Some work at night. Some work on weekends. They are often on call for emergencies. Some officers are part of a city's police department.

ANIMAL COPS

Animal cops protect animals. They can arrest people who hurt animals. They can give people fines.

Sometimes officers visit the animal shelter to check on the animals they rescued.

An officer feeds a rescued sea turtle.

The work can be difficult. Some animals are sick or hurt. Some do not survive. But animal control officers try to help as many animals as they can. They try to keep animals safe. Each animal they help makes a difference.

Officers rescue wild animals, such as deer.

GLOSSARY

certificate
an official document that people can earn by demonstrating a specific skill

patrol
to protect an area by making regular trips through it

rewarding
worthwhile; making a person feel he or she has done something good and important

stray
an animal that has wandered away from home or is homeless

testify
to give facts in a court of law

vet
an animal doctor

OTHER JOBS TO CONSIDER

ANIMAL SHELTER WORKER

Animal shelter workers care for animals that stay in a shelter. They feed, clean, and play with the animals.

VETERINARIAN

Veterinarians are doctors for animals. They take care of sick or hurt animals. They help animals stay healthy. Some focus on pets. Other vets might focus on farm animals or wild animals.

VETERINARY TECHNICIAN

Veterinary technicians help veterinarians. They help examine animals. They may give animals shots and treatments. They may run lab tests.

ACTIVITY

KEEPING ANIMALS SAFE

Animal control officers pick up many stray animals. But pet owners can help keep their pets from becoming strays. They can help keep their pets safe at home. Some build fences around their yards. Others put collars on their pets. The collars have the owner's contact information on them.

Think about different ways owners can keep their pets safe. How can they keep their pets from wandering from home? Search online for ideas. Make a poster or handout about what you find. Share that information with your neighborhood. You can ask to post the information at your local animal shelter.

FURTHER RESOURCES

**Curious about other jobs with animals?
Learn more here:**

American Humane Society: Ways to Help Animals as a Career
http://site.americanhumane.org/kids/career.htm

Bedell, J. M. *So, You Want to Work with Animals? Discover Fantastic Ways to Work with Animals, from Veterinary Science to Aquatic Biology.* New York: Aladdin, 2017.

Guillain, Charlotte. *Animals.* Chicago, Ill.: Heinemann Library, 2013.

Want to help animals now? Check out this resource:

Angels Among Us Pet Rescue: 10 Ways Children Can Help Animal Shelters
www.angelsrescue.org/volunteer/just-for-kids/

INDEX